The Official Arsenal Yearbook 1993

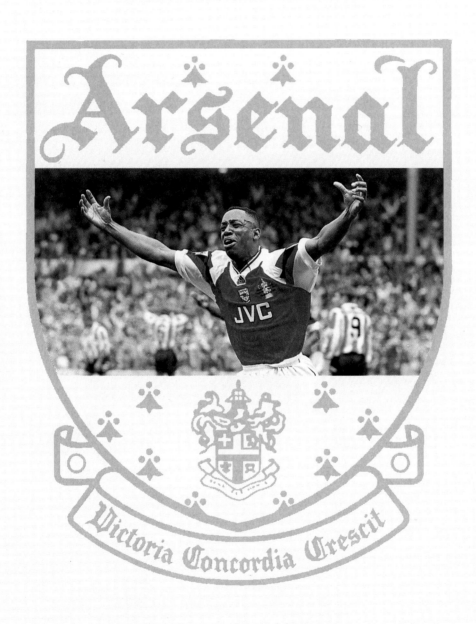

THE OFFICIAL
ARSENAL
YEARBOOK 1993

Kevin Connolly

Foreword by Tony Adams

HAMLYN

CONTENTS

First published in Great Britain
in 1993 by Hamlyn,
an imprint of
Reed Consumer Books Limited
Michelin House, 81 Fulham Road,
London SW3 6RB
and Auckland, Melbourne,
Singapore and Toronto

Copyright © 1993 Reed International
Books Limited

Design: Four Corners, London

A catalogue record for this book is
available from the British Library

ISBN 0 600 57948 4

Printed and bound in Great Britain by
BPCC Hazell Books Ltd
Member of BPCC Ltd

PHOTOGRAPHIC ACKNOWLEDGEMENTS

All pictures supplied by Colorsport except
the following: Action-Plus: 5 left; Allsport:
front cover; Arsenal FC Museum: 55 top;
Arsenal FC/Doug Poole: 55 bottom;
John Babb: 2-3, 6, 24, 25 top right, 30, 32,
35 bottom, 36, 36-37, 37, 46-47, 49, 51;
Empics/Paul Marriott: 6-7; S & G Press
Agency Ltd: 58-59, 58 inset; Bill Smith: 7,
9, 26, 28 bottom, 28 inset, 29, 38, 48 right,
53 left, 53 right.

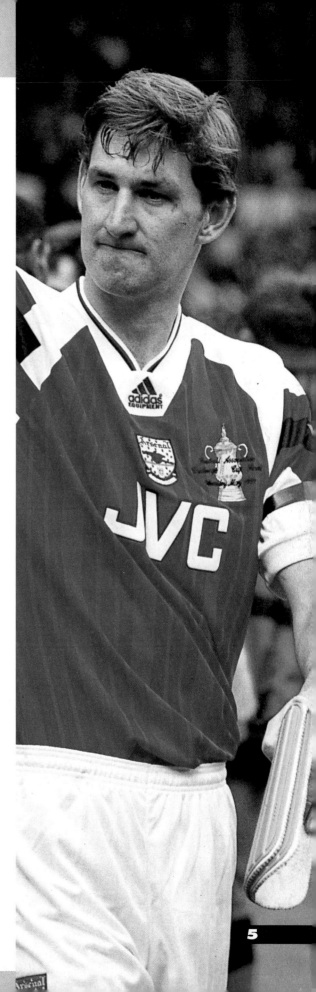

IT WAS A FANTASTIC FEELING . . . lifting the F.A. Cup at Wembley to add to the Coca Cola Cup the month before: a piece of history which will be hard to match.

So many memories . . . edging through on penalties against Millwall; the battle at the Baseball Ground before we overcame Derby in the replay; coming from behind in the Coca Cola final; travelling to Yeovil in the F.A. Cup, knowing so many people were willing us to lose; two displays of huge resilience against Leeds; Ian Wright's goals against Forest.

The quarter-final win at Ipswich was probably our best performance. And I'll never forget heading the winner against Spurs at Wembley. That was sweet revenge for 1991.

The final was a slog between two tired teams. Overall, I thought we just about deserved it – and Andy Lininghan's last minute winner reminded me of Michael Thomas' goal at Anfield in 1989!

Yet, even as we were celebrating a wonderful end to a memorable season, we were thinking ahead to 1993/4.

We've just had our worst League season for years. That's not good enough, especially after we started Premier League title favourites. We went 17 cup games unbeaten. That's the consistency we have to re-discover in the League. We have the players to do it.

That's the challenge ahead.

And Europe too. I've said many times, how much the European Cup defeat by Benfica hurt. That's a memory we want to wipe out.

We know our supporters have high expectations. That's what a club of Arsenal's reputation is all about.

We hope you'll have plenty to enjoy in 1993/4.

Meanwhile, I hope you enjoy this book!

Tony Adams

BUILDING THE STAND OF THE FUTURE

Norwest Holst

ARSENAL FOOTBALL CLUB
WELCOMES ITS MAIN SPONSORS

JVC
CITROËN
SHOOTING STARS
Chrysalis Home Video

adidas
CLUBCALL 0898 20202
Lucozade
LADBROKES

HIGHBURY looked like a building site throughout 1992/3. But by the autumn of 1993, Arsenal Stadium will be complete again – and one of the most modern in Europe. The stadium had to be re-built to comply with the Taylor Report's recommendations. Now Arsenal will be all-seat ten months before Taylor's August 1994 deadline.

ABOVE LEFT: An artist's impression of the new North Bank Stand.

MAIN PICTURE: The impressive old North Bank.

BELOW: The builders move in on the North Bank.

The symbol of Highbury's rebuilding throughout 1992-1993 was the mural which covered the old North Bank end.

The North Bank had been demolished at the end of the previous season. A gigantic 12,000 seat North Bank Stand, costing £16.5 million, has risen in its place, ready for the start of 1993/4. The new stand is among the most impressive this side of the Atlantic, with bars, restaurants, video screens, the Arsenal Museum and its own creche.

Work on converting the West Stand Paddock began in January and was completed two months later. The 1,542-seat development opened in time for the Coca Cola Cup semi-final second leg against Crystal Palace on March 10.

REBUILDING THE CLOCK END

That left the Clock End, plus the East Stand Paddock, where the Junior Gunners stood.

Reconstruction started in May, straight after David O'Leary's testimonial. The building work will be finished in the autumn. It could have been completed earlier – if Arsenal had simply bolted seats to existing terracing.

'We didn't do that because of the lines of sight,' said managing director Ken Friar. So the banking has been re-tiered so everyone can see clearly.

The total re-development will cost £22.5 million. When it's completed, Highbury's capacity will rise to around 40,000. And – just like when Herbert Chapman initiated the great re-building programme of the 1930s – Arsenal Stadium will be one of the finest in Europe.

THE GUNNERS

'HERE WE GO, HERE WE GO, HERE WE GO . . .' Optimism reigned as the Gunners opened their challenge for the Premier League championship against unfancied Norwich at North Bank-less Highbury.

Fans favourite David Rocastle had been sold to Leeds for £2 million a few weeks earlier. However, George Graham had signed one of Denmark's European championship-winning heroes – John Jensen, from Brondby for £1.1million. Arsenal started 2-1 title favourites. Ridiculous odds, doubtless inspired by the Gunners' 17- game unbeaten finish to 1991/2.

Things started well enough. Steve Bould headed home a free kick. Kevin Campbell netted a second before half time. The red-and-white army was on the march.

EARLY JOLTS

But Norwich forgot to read the script. David Seaman and Tony Adams were still contemplating the new back pass rule. Mark Robins and David Phillips levelled. Ruel Fox and Robins, again, sent the rest of the ground as quiet as the mural. 'Oh, I say!' as John Motson might have remarked in the circumstances . . .

Blackburn continued the poor start. Alan Shearer barged over Jimmy Carter and ran on to strike a shot that flew off an anti-Arsenal divot and stranded Seaman.

'Crisis at Highbury,' ran the

adidas · adidas

ClubCall 0898-20 20 20
CALLS CHARGED AT 36p PER MIN. CHEAP · 48p ALL OTHER TIMES

BELOW RIGHT: David Hillier, Anders Limpar and Lee Dixon greet new boy John Jensen.

BELOW LEFT: The first of many?! Steve Bould heads Arsenal in front against Norwich.

RIGHT: Celebration time! Lee Dixon congratulates Ray Parlour after Ray had thumped Arsenal into an eighth minute lead against Sheffield Wednesday.

headlines, as the Gunners travelled to Anfield. In came Ray Parlour for Paul Merson. Parlour set up the opening goal for Anders Limpar, then supplied the pass for Ian Wright to hit the second. Arsenal's show was back on the road.

Northern Ireland defender Stephen Morrow replaced Jensen (away on World Cup duty) when the Gunners

brushed off Oldham 2-0 with goals by Nigel Winterburn and Wright. The Dane returned for a 2-1 win over Sheffield Wednesday. Parlour struck an early cracker. Then the new, lightweight Merson hit the second.

However, there was growing press speculation about the team. Were the Gunners giving their forwards enough supply? Did Arsenal have the midfield spark to win the title?

PREMIER LEAGUE RESULTS

AUGUST 15

Arsenal 2
Bould, Campbell

Norwich City 4
Robins 2, Phillips, Fox

AUGUST 18

Blackburn Rovers 1
Shearer

Arsenal 0

AUGUST 23

Liverpool 0

Arsenal 2
Limpar, Wright

AUGUST 26

Arsenal 2
Winterburn, Wright

Oldham 0

AUGUST 29

Arsenal 2
Parlour, Merson

Sheffield Wed. 1
Hirst

LEAGUE POSITION

Pld	W	D	L	F	A	Pts	Pos
5	3	0	2	8	6	9	4th

AN UP AND DOWN MONTH

THE MONTH OPENED with a disappointing and bruising 0-0 draw at QPR. Chances were few and far between. The poor ball spent most of the time hurtling through the air.

PREMIER LEAGUE RESULTS

SEPTEMBER 2

Queens Park Rangers 0	Arsenal 0

SEPTEMBER 5

Wimbledon 3	Arsenal 2
Sanchez, Fashanu, Earle	Wright 2

SEPTEMBER 12

Arsenal 0	Blackburn Rovers 1
	Newell

SEPTEMBER 19

Sheffield United 1	Arsenal 1
Whitehouse	Wright

SEPTEMBER 28

Arsenal 1	Manchester City 0
Wright	

LEAGUE POSITION

Pld	W	D	L	F	A	Pts	Pos
10	4	2	4	12	11	14	9th

It was more of the same when the Gunners lost to Wimbledon at Selhurst Park. The ball probably needed half-a-dozen Anadin after the bashing it took. Whoever said football was a game best played on the ground?

Ian Wright tucked Arsenal in front. Lawrie Sanchez equalised after a goalmouth melee. Tony Adams had to go off with a cut. The Dons scored a minute later. Wright nodded his second within 60 seconds. Never mind the quality. . . feel the excitement? But there was no happy ending for the 8,000 travelling Arsenal fans. Robbie Earle smacked home a 20-yard winner, three minutes from the final whistle.

QUESTIONS ARE ASKED

Defeat at home to Blackburn deepened the surrounding gloom. 18-year-old Ian Selley made his debut, replacing suspended David Hillier. Even the 77th minute introduction of Kevin Campbell never looked like breaking down a packed defence.

'Crisis at Highbury' headlines erupted again. So did the queries about Limpar, who, although available, started only one League game throughout the month.

Speculation about Arsenal's midfield grew. Jensen was adjusting to the pace of English football and to playing so many games in such a short time

Limpar and Merson were both

substituted after Arsenal fell behind at Bramall Lane. On came centre back Andy Linighan and debut-making Mark Flatts. Wright equalised. George Graham declared that sometimes he had to adopt a pragmatic approach to pick up points.

THE MANAGER ANSWERS

There were changes for the game against Manchester City. Graham plumped for Campbell, Alan Smith and Wright up front, with Paul Merson 'floating' behind them.

Wright netted the only goal – Arsenal's first at the Mural End. The 'Curse of the Mural' was lifted. Limpar came on to a hero's welcome, to be floored by Steve McMahon within a few minutes.

But Arsenal had found a formation to tide them over.

ABOVE RIGHT: Two big signings in competition . . . John Jensen tussles with Blackburn's Alan Shearer.

BELOW RIGHT: Paul Merson and Steve Bould congratulate Ian Wright on opening the scoring against Wimbledon at Selhurst Park.

BACKGROUND: Sky Sports' razzamatazz comes to Highbury!

'One Tony Adams . . . There's only one Tony Adams . . .' The words rang around Wembley after the Arsenal skipper headed the goal that knocked out Tottenham in the F.A. Cup semi-final.

BELOW: Tony scores the Wembley winner against Tottenham.

RIGHT: Tony celebrates after the Wembley win over Spurs.

If Ian Wright's goals powered Arsenal towards Wembley on two fronts, then Adams was the driving force behind the Gunners' assaults.

He was outstanding: strong, resolute, virtually unbeatable in the air – and very, very hard to pass. No wonder he won back his England place.

If you need someone alongside you in a battle, Tony would head the list of candidates. He proved that when England had to show nerve as well as ability to complete a World Cup win in Turkey when too many of the home crowd behaved like hooligans. Adams kept playing and kept leading.

ROCK OF DEFENCE

George Graham made the then-21-year-old Adams his captain in March 1988 – and Arsenal have stuck by Tony through thick and thin.

Sometimes it's hard to believe the accident-prone Adams is the same giant who's achieved so much on the football pitch.

1992/3 provided some prize examples. There was Adams, falling down some steps, being carted off to Bart's Hospital – and needing 29 stitches in a head wound which kept him out of League games at Chelsea and Norwich. And there was Tony, a week later, forehead dressed, heading the equaliser which set the Gunners on the way to that 4-2 F.A. Cup quarter-final triumph at Ipswich.

There was Adams, nodding the winner against Arsenal's greatest rivals on April 4. There was Adams, lifting the Coca Cola Cup two weeks later.

Hurt Adams, and for all his brave face – his insistence that he doesn't read the critics – he bleeds. But there's no harder man in English football. The more he's attacked, the stronger he bounces back.

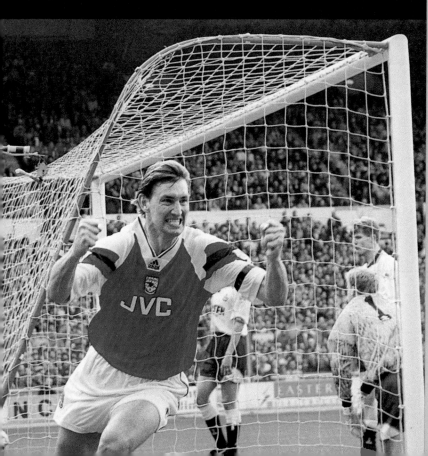

Tony Adams

THREE GAMES, THREE WINS!

OCTOBER WAS BLISS . . . three League wins and a maximum of nine points. But some question marks remained. The Gunners were winning, yet rarely killing off opponents with the certainty that marked the end of 1991/2.

A lan Smith, Ian Wright and Kevin Campbell continued up front. Merson stung from just behind. The position suited Merse, who enjoyed a 'free' midfield role. The 'diamond' formation, it was dubbed. With Smith as spearhead, and Merson coming from deep, it proved too sharp for unsuspecting opponents.

The Chelsea game was almost a bad joke. Merson stroked a brilliant lob to put Arsenal ahead. The Gunners should have been four or five up before Denis Wise scrambled an equaliser. Dixon had a penalty saved. Enter Limpar. It wasn't long before he dodged round Gareth Hall and crossed for Wright to nick the winner.

IN CONTROL . . . BUT IT'S NO STROLL

The Gunners had controlled the game so much, they should have been strolling. That concerned George Graham, as much as the crowd. It became a theme for the league season.

Everyone celebrated a 1-0 win at Nottingham Forest a fortnight later though. Alan Smith's first goal of the season proved decisive. Hillier and Winterburn were outstanding. Gary Crosby's shot against the post was Forest's only effort on target. But Arsenal could

have won by more again.

It was the same against Everton. An injury to Nigel Winterburn – after the Gunners had used both subs – proved a cruel blow. Yet once more Arsenal could have added to the two scored by Wright and 38th minute substitute Limpar, who beat Neville Southall with an exquisite lob. David Seaman made two vital saves from Tony Cottee in the last ten minutes too.

Winterburn's ligament injury kept him out for six games before he returned in the derby at Tottenham the following month.

PREMIER LEAGUE RESULTS

OCTOBER 3	
Arsenal 2	**Chelsea 1**
Merson, Wright	Wise

OCTOBER 17	
Nottingham Forest 0	**Arsenal 1** Smith

OCTOBER 24	
Arsenal 2	**Everton 0**
Wright, Limpar	

LEAGUE POSITION

Pld	W	D	L	F	A	Pts	Pos
13	7	2	4	17	12	23	**4th**

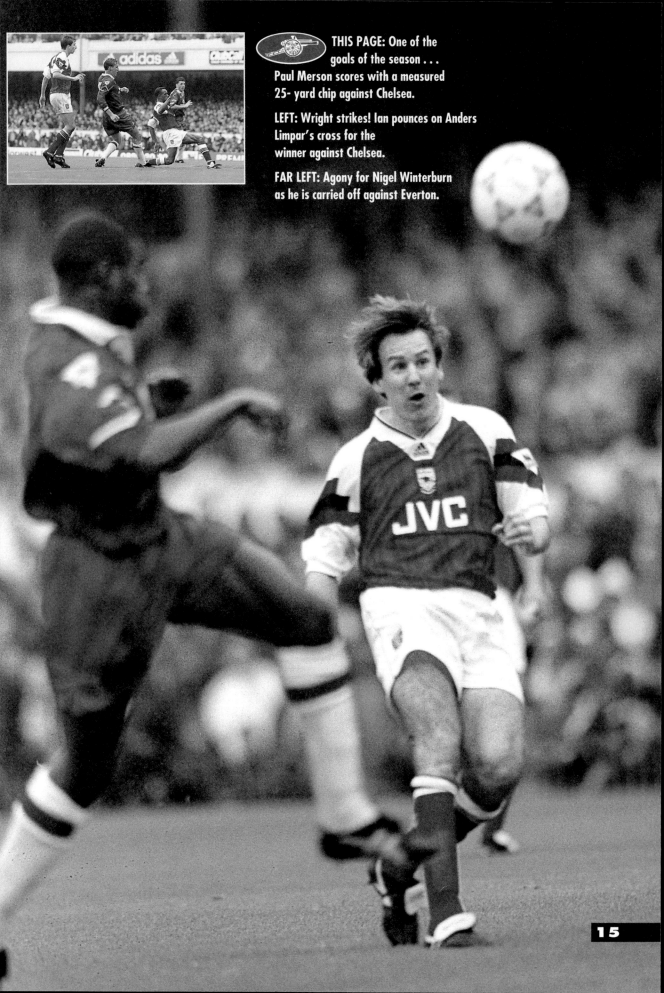

THIS PAGE: One of the goals of the season . . . Paul Merson scores with a measured 25- yard chip against Chelsea.

LEFT: Wright strikes! Ian pounces on Anders Limpar's cross for the winner against Chelsea.

FAR LEFT: Agony for Nigel Winterburn as he is carried off against Everton.

BACK DOWN TO EARTH

ARSENAL ROARED INTO November like lions and came out of it like lambs. Sky's cameras had proved happy mascots, so far. They televised another Arsenal success away from home, at Crystal Palace.

PREMIER LEAGUE RESULTS

NOVEMBER 2

Crystal Palace 1	Arsenal 2
McGoldrick	Merson, Wright

NOVEMBER 7

Arsenal 3	Coventry City 0
Smith, Wright, Campbell	

NOVEMBER 21

Leeds United 3	Arsenal 0
Fairclough, Chapman, McAllister	

NOVEMBER 28

Arsenal 0	Manchester United 1
	Hughes

LEAGUE POSITION

Pld	W	D	L	F	A	Pts	Pos
17	9	2	6	22	17	29	3rd

Stephen Morrow deputised at left back for injured Nigel Winterburn and grew more confident by the minute. Paul Merson blasted the Gunners into an early lead. Eddie McGoldrick levelled. Then Ian Wright pounced, to destroy the club where he built his reputation.

Alan Smith reached a landmark when Arsenal thrashed Coventry 3-0. His eighth minute goal made him only the 13th Gunner to score 100 for the club. Wright crashed a blinding second. Campbell made it three on the stroke of half time.

Arsenal, Arsenal, top of the league,' sang the old North Bankers on the Clock End when Joe Worrall blew the final whistle.

For two days, and a few hours, George Graham's men headed the Premier League – until Norwich won 3-2 at Oldham that Monday night.

Never mind: Arsenal were firmly installed as title favourites. Six wins on the trot. The Gunners were going to turn the race into

a procession, like they'd done in 1991. But Smith, the vital target man, was out, nursing a stress fracture.

NEXT STOP LEEDS

Arsenal then travelled to Leeds, still smarting from their European Cup defeat by Rangers. A bomb scare forced them out of bed at 4.30 in the morning. It was an omen. David Seaman was injured after 51 minutes. The Gunners had just fallen behind to Chris Fairclough's header. Lee Chapman and Gary McAllister piled on the agony.

Normal service was to be resumed against Manchester United. Only Mark Hughes spoiled the revival with the only goal of the game, and Ryan Giggs led Arsenal a dance.

MAIN PICTURE: TV spectacular . . . Ian Wright smacks the winner against Crystal Palace.

FAR LEFT: Tony Adams tussles with Lee Chapman during the defeat at Elland Road.

LEFT: Arsenal's first-ever sub goalie in a League match, Alan Miller, who replaced injured David Seaman at Leeds.

The Wright to STRIKE!

It's 50-odd years since Arsenal have had a striker like Ian Wright. Older fans will remember centre forward Ted Drake. Only Drake's 136 goals in 182 games boasts a higher scoring ratio than Wright's 56 goals in 79 outings.

Comparisons down the years are always dodgy. But Wright has netted his goals when it's never been harder to score, including one each to put Arsenal ahead in the F.A. Cup final and replay.

Wright dedicated his replay goal to ex-Crystal Palace manager Steve Coppell, the man who gave Ian his chance in football. Coppell and staff plucked Wright from park football to become a household name. But Arsenal's record £2.5 million signing is well aware of the Gunners history.

'It's a great honour to be compared with Ted Drake. I've been here less than two seasons. They've been great, but there's a long way to go yet,' says Ian, whose goal on May 8, helped relegate his old club to the First Division. Ian was sorry about that. He's still friends with several Palace players.

PLAYING THROUGH PAIN

Doing the business in the F.A. Cup final was his main objective. He did it too, despite painkilling injections for a toe injury and an ankle knock which forced him off after 90 minutes in the opening game – and nine minutes earlier in the replay.

That wasn't the first time Wright's goals have almost decided a Cup final. His double as a substitute almost wrecked Manchester United in 1990. United gained a 3-3 draw, then snatched the replay, 1-0.

His replay opener against Wednesday was his 30th of the season – more than any other Premier League striker. And he missed 11 games through injury and suspension.

'I always thought the move to Arsenal would do me good, because it would give me more chances,' says Wright. Coca Cola Cup. F.A. Cup. What next?!

RIGHT: Ian, and the F.A. Cup!

'I've had a lot to prove in a short space of time. I came late into the pro game. I was nearly 28 when I joined Arsenal. But there's a lot more I can still achieve.'

THE YOUNG ONES

Ray Parlour, Stephen Morrow and Ian Selley have proved that. Mark Flatts made a promising first team start too.

England under-21 winger Neil Heaney and Scotland under-21 forward Paul Dickov are waiting in the wings, along with defender Scott Marshall, striker Paul Shaw and ex-youth team topscorer Paul Read, whose progress last season was wrecked by ruptured knee ligaments.

Another crop of home-grown youngsters burst into the limelight in 1992/3 – in the Arsenal tradition. The Gunners justly claim that no club can match their record of gaining top honours with a core of players who've risen through the ranks.

NEW BOYS

Parlour started six League games in 1991/2. But he made his mark with a vengeance at Anfield last August, playing a part in both goals as the Gunners beat Liverpool 2-0. He cracked a stunning shot six days later to set us on the way to victory over Sheffield Wednesday and that set up the 20 year-old from Romford for an exciting season.'If you said to me last August that I'd be an established member of the first team squad, I'd have been satisfied with that. To play in so many important cup ties was an extra thrill,' said Parlour.

At the start of the season, Morrow wondered whether he had a Highbury future. He'd played more matches for Northern Ireland than for Arsenal. Now he's signed a new contract and become a valuable member of the Gunners squad. 'I thought maybe I'd have to move on to gain first team football. But the last few months have been the best of my time here,' said 23 year-old Morrow, who deputised when Nigel Winterburn was injured last November. Then he switched to a midfield marking role, snuffing out many dangerous opponents .

Selley was an 18 year-old unknown just out of the youth team, when he made his debut against Blackburn last September. Since then, he's played in Coca Cola and F.A. Cup triumphs and turned out at Wembley. He'd have made even more first team appearances but for a trip with England to the World Youth Cup finals in Australia.

Tricky winger Flatts quickly won over the Highbury fans with his intricate skills. He was hampered by injury after a sparkling display in the 1-0 win at Manchester City in January. He's another to watch in 1993/4!

LEFT TO RIGHT:
Stephen Morrow,
Ray Parlour and Ian Selley

NOT MUCH

CHRISTMAS CHEER

TWO POINTS from five matches savaged Arsenal's title hopes. Key players, such as Davis and Limpar, were absent through injury. The Gunners' losing run continued at Southampton, where Ian Wright missed a late penalty and Lee Dixon departed with a hamstring injury after 25 minutes.

RIGHT: Andy's younger brother, David Linighan, is shadowed by Steve Bould in the game against Ipswich.

FAR RIGHT: Anders Limpar fires in a cross despite the close attention of Aston Villa's Earl Barrett.

A week later, all hell broke loose as Tottenham won the north London derby. Wright's alleged off-the-ball incident with David Howells cost him a three match ban. But Arsenal fans still seethe about ref Alf Buksh, who turned down two blatant penalties, the first when Ray Parlour was legged up in the second minute, and the other when Paul Merson was fouled in the second half.

GUNNERS LOSE THEIR GRIP

Arsenal aimed to end their losing run against Middlesbrough. The fans endured another bout of frustration. A mix-up between Andy Linighan and David Seaman gifted Boro' a 34th minute lead. It was nine minutes from time when Wright managed to pull it back.

Boxing Day against Ipswich was a major disappointment. They kept ten men behind the ball and stifled the game. Ipswich got away with it, just. Wright raced past four challenges and cracked a diagonal shot past Clive Baker, only to groan as the ball bounced off a post and rolled along the line.

At Aston Villa, Sky's cameras were anything but lucky mascots. With Tony Adams on the second match of his suspension, George Graham used David O'Leary behind Steve Bould and Linighan, for his first start of the season.

It was O'Leary's challenge on Dwight Yorke which conceded the penalty that decided the match. Graham rated the performance on a par with the disaster at Leeds, though Arsenal livened up with Limpar's arrival after 66 minutes.

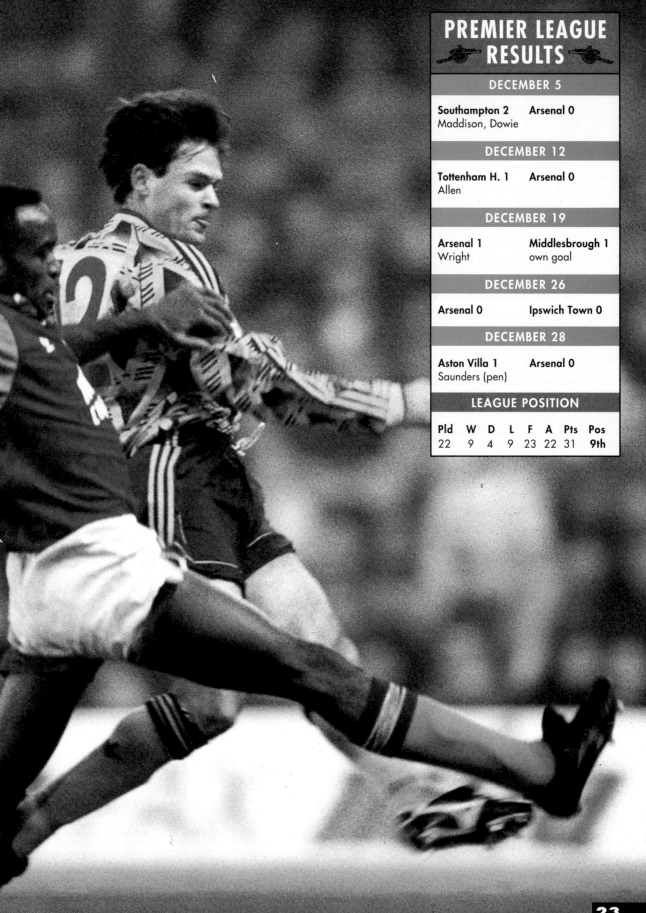

PREMIER LEAGUE RESULTS

DECEMBER 5

Southampton 2   **Arsenal 0**
Maddison, Dowie

DECEMBER 12

Tottenham H. 1   **Arsenal 0**
Allen

DECEMBER 19

Arsenal 1   **Middlesbrough 1**
Wright   own goal

DECEMBER 26

Arsenal 0   **Ipswich Town 0**

DECEMBER 28

Aston Villa 1   **Arsenal 0**
Saunders (pen)

LEAGUE POSITION

Pld	W	D	L	F	A	Pts	Pos
22	9	4	9	23	22	31	**9th**

NEW YEAR RESOLUTION

ARSENAL WERE progressing in the cups. The league was a different story. Steve Bould was the third Gunner to be suspended in 1992/3. So Andy Linighan stepped in against struggling Sheffield United.

David Hillier lashed his first goal of the season. Arsenal were romping away. Only they couldn't add another goal. Three minutes from time, Adrian Littlejohn swooped on a Linighan error and equalised.

George Graham and Tony Adams were to call on the crowd for louder support – with mixed response. Ian Wright started his three match ban when Arsenal travelled to Manchester City. In came Kevin Campbell, plus Mark Flatts for the injured Limpar.

INJURIES AND SUSPENSIONS SAP GUNNERS STRENGTH

Flatts and Paul Merson, ensconsced on the wing again, were the matchwinners. Flatts tormented Terry Phelan. Merson met one of his crosses close in to net the Gunners 79th minute winner.

Arsenal were buoyant. There was even talk of a late run to snatch the title. Yet injuries and suspensions were taking their toll. Limpar, Flatts and Bould were all

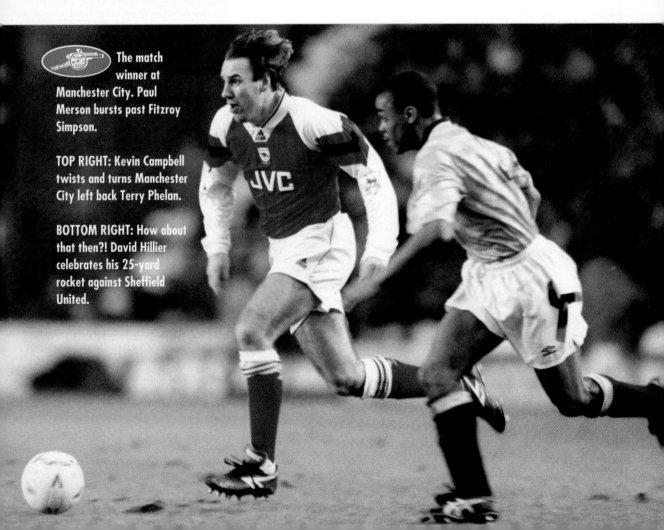

The match winner at Manchester City. Paul Merson bursts past Fitzroy Simpson.

TOP RIGHT: Kevin Campbell twists and turns Manchester City left back Terry Phelan.

BOTTOM RIGHT: How about that then?! David Hillier celebrates his 25-yard rocket against Sheffield United.

recovering, when Liverpool visited Highbury for another Sky live game. John Jensen had started a two-game ban. Wright was serving his last match.

Jimmy Carter began his second game of the season. Ray Parlour lined up alongside David Hillier. Paul Stewart fouled Hillier early and often. He was booked. Hillier had to leave after 12 minutes, with a 'dead leg.' Paul Merson supplied most of Arsenal's ideas, though chances were rare. Nigel Winterburn was booked for upending Steve McManaman.

SPOTS OF BOTHER

It was a tale of two penalties. Linighan pulled back Ian Rush and John Barnes scored. Minutes later, Campbell was sent flying but Merson whacked his spot kick too close to David James.

It was the third missed penalty of the season in the league following Lee Dixon and Wright's misses.

Worse followed. Winterburn was sent off for a second foul on McManaman in an unfortunate ending to the game.

PREMIER LEAGUE RESULTS

JANUARY 9	
Arsenal 1	**Sheffield United 1**
Hillier	Littlejohn

JANUARY 16	
Manchester City 0	**Arsenal 1**
	Merson

JANUARY 31	
Arsenal 0	**Liverpool 1**
	Barnes (pen)

LEAGUE POSITION

Pld	W	D	L	F	A	Pts	Pos
25	10	5	10	25	24	35	11th

David O'Leary's

LAST HURRAH

When George Graham announced on March 19 that Arsenal were giving their appearance record holder a free transfer in

Not even fairytale genius Hans Christian Andersen could have scripted David O'Leary's finale, after a magical 20-year Arsenal career.

recognition of his service, Highbury fans assumed they'd seen the end of an era. The Ireland centre half would fade out gracefully, before a well-deserved farewell match on May 17.

Sometimes though, the good guys do get their rewards. It was cruel on Lee Dixon that suspension ruled him out of the Coca Cola Cup final. In stepped O'Leary. Right back was never David's position. But you'd never have guessed that as he grew in confidence throughout the second half. And how the Arsenal fans roared when he lifted the cup. A grand ending? 'You ain't seen nothin' yet!'

Come the F.A. Cup final, and he's on the bench. Wright is injured. But George Graham knows exactly what to do next – send on O'Leary! Suddenly Arsenal look tighter.

Extra time doesn't produce a winner. So there we are again the following Thursday night. This time Wrighty's toe and ankle injuries force him off after 81 minutes. Enter O'Leary again. And Wednesday don't have another decent shot on target.

Between these two Wembley occasions was O'Leary's 'farewell' against League champions Manchester United. Beautifully scripted again: a 4-4 draw, with O'Leary hitting Arsenal's equaliser. And 22,117 fans turned out to support O'Leary.

When will we see his like again?

ABOVE RIGHT: What a way to finish! David raises the F.A. Cup aloft.

RIGHT: O'Leary on Wembley duty in the Coca Cola Cup final.

LEFT: David before his 'farewell' match, with children John and Ciara and Manchester United skipper Bryan Robson.

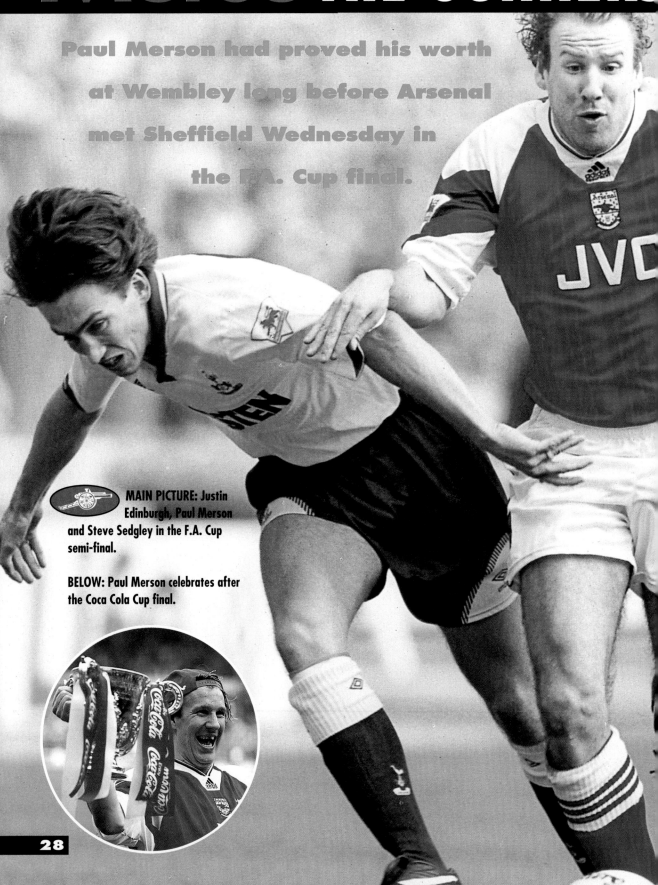

Merse THE GUNNERS

Paul Merson had proved his worth
at Wembley long before Arsenal
met Sheffield Wednesday in
the F.A. Cup final.

MAIN PICTURE: Justin
Edinburgh, Paul Merson
and Steve Sedgley in the F.A. Cup
semi-final.

BELOW: Paul Merson celebrates after
the Coca Cola Cup final.

Trevor Francis's team had already seen more than enough of the 25-year-old Gunner, when Arsenal pipped Sheffield Wednesday 2-1 in the Coca Cola Cup final.

'I was happier with my form in the Coca Cola at Wembley than in the two F.A. Cup finals,' admitted Merson with typical bluntness. 'I was rubbish in the first F.A. Cup final.'

In the replay, he saw two shots saved low down by Chris Woods, before earning his first F.A. Cup winners medal. But the Coca Cola was his finest hour.

FAITH REWARDED

Paul was sure the Gunners would triumph – even when Wednesday went ahead. 'I always felt it was going to be our day,' he recalls.

Merson's 25-yard cracker launched Arsenal back. His runs at Roland Nilsson – and teasing of the Owls defence – earned him well-deserved star billing that April afternoon.

'I work all the time on shots like that. Sometimes they go in. Other times they're more likely to take someone's head off at the back of the stand!'

That was Merse's reply when asked about the cracking 25-yarder that kept Arsenal in the F.A. Cup after Leeds had cruised to a 2-0 lead in the fourth round at Highbury. Those who saw his magnificent chip against Chelsea or the majestic free kick winner in the league at Ipswich, know practice and skill have paid off.

Yet Merson would prefer a few more 'ordinary' goals.

'I'd swop one memorable goal for three tap-ins,' he says. 'I score some great goals, but I'd rather have more to my name at the end of a season.'

GEORGE STRENGTHENS THE SQUAD

THIS WAS THE MONTH when Arsenal's lingering championship hopes finally died – killed by those spoil-sports from Wimbledon.

It was the month when George Graham paid Everton £2 million to re-sign Martin Keown, the England centre back who had left Highbury for Aston Villa shortly after Graham's arrival in 1986.

It was also the month when injuries started to bite. Steve Bould was sidelined with a pulled thigh. Lee Dixon missed all three league games because of knocks. An ankle injury kept out Ray Parlour. Ligament problems hampered Mark Flatts. Alan Smith, just recalled to the England squad, limped off with a twisted ankle against the Dons. Ian Wright couldn't play at Oldham.

And February ended disastrously for John Jensen. He gave up on Denmark's trip to Argentina, to play for Arsenal. Two days before the Leeds game, he went down with a groin injury in training.

The three league matches are best forgotten – grim anti-climaxes after the cup excitement.

KEOWN'S SECOND DEBUT

Keown made his second Arsenal 'debut', deputising for Dixon against the Dons. Once more, the ball spent most of the game flying through the air, but Dean Holdsworth grabbed the game's only goal, after 20 minutes.

Premier League title dreams became but a distant memory for the pre-season favourites. There was even talk of Arsenal slipping towards the relegation zone.

That lent an extra significance to the Gunners' trip to Oldham, where they'd never won. Six players were out. Dixon, Wright and Smith were sidelined. Steve Morrow replaced suspended Nigel Winterburn. Bould and Parlour were starting in the reserves.

Andy Linighan, so long the butt of the boo-boys in the Highbury crowd, headed Arsenal's 50th minute winner and sent his old club to the bottom of the table.

Leeds had crashed 0-5 at Tottenham the same day. They weren't going to get stuffed like that again. Howard Wilkinson's team sat nine men behind the ball and the Gunners couldn't break them down. It might have been different, if Wright's second minute 'goal' hadn't been inexplicably disallowed. Arsenal hadn't won a league match at Highbury since November 7.

PREMIER LEAGUE RESULTS

FEBRUARY 10

Arsenal 0	Wimbledon 1
	Holdsworth

FEBRUARY 20

Oldham 0	Arsenal 1
	Linighan

FEBRUARY 24

Arsenal 0	Leeds 0

LEAGUE POSITION

Pld	W	D	L	F	A	Pts	Pos
28	11	6	11	26	25	39	11th

FAR RIGHT: Alan Smith, in a tangle with Wimbledon's Robbie Earle.

RIGHT: Goal scorer Andy Linighan salutes Arsenal's travelling fans after heading the winner at Oldham.

A Gunner Again!

KEOWN returns to Highbury

Martin Keown rejoined Arsenal in February. Though he couldn't play in the Gunners' cup games, the England centre back is looking forward to years of success ahead.

It was December 1985 when the 19-year-old Keown made his Arsenal debut in a 2-0 win over Liverpool, a few weeks after returning from a loan spell at Brighton.

He played 27 games for Arsenal, then left at the end of the season to join Aston Villa.

'Having spent nearly four years at Arsenal and finally reaching the first team, it was a bit of a wrench to leave for another club,' recalls Keown.

Keown later moved to Everton in a deal worth £750,000, and won nine caps for England. But the Oxford-born defender remained a Gunner at heart.

HIGHBURY – WHERE THE HEART IS

'When I first returned to Highbury with Villa, I found it hard. Playing against players you know is not easy. And when you've cleaned out the toilets and done all the odd jobs as an apprentice, there's bound to be some of the club running through your blood,' he says.

So when Martin heard about George Graham's approach, he didn't think long before moving back to his football roots.

'I didn't need much time to make up my mind. I had good times with Villa and Everton, but my heart is really at Highbury,' says Keown.

Martin made his opening appearances at right back, deputising for Lee Dixon. But the pacy defender is earmarked for a covering centre back role, alongside his old youth team partner, Tony Adams.

That takes Keown back to Arsenal's 1983/4 side who reached the F.A. Youth Cup semi-final. In the team were Gus Caesar and Michael Thomas at full back; David Rocastle in midfield; Niall Quinn and Martin Hayes up front – plus a centre back pairing of Keown and Adams!

'Tony and I seemed to take steps together,' recalls Martin. 'He attacked the ball. I tidied up behind. It worked well. We had a nice balance.

'We can do that again. I went close to the championship with Villa. But Tony has won two titles with Arsenal. I hope I can join him in another one – and get back into the England team alongside him.'

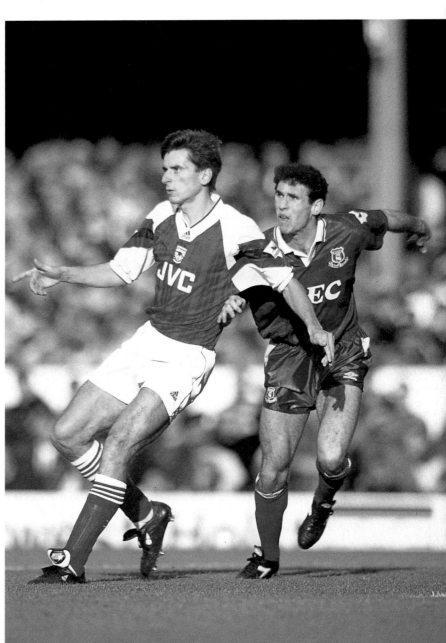

THE GUNNERS GET
STRONGER

ARSENAL started March slowly – then grew stronger and stronger. Reaching the Coca Cola Cup final and the F.A. Cup semi-final were highlights to remember. But the Gunners also defied a mounting fixture list to climb the Premier League table.

TOP RIGHT: Jimmy Carter, the match winner against Southampton.

RIGHT: Paul Dickov, against Southampton in his Premier League debut

BELOW RIGHT: Kevin Campbell and Paul Merson congratulate Ian Wright, after his goal at Coventry.

Skipper Tony Adams missed the opening matches too, after falling downstairs and needing 29 stitches in a cut head.

Yet Arsenal's only defeat came at bogey ground Stamford Bridge on March 1. The Gunners hadn't beaten Chelsea there since 1974.

Two days later Arsenal visited title-chasing Norwich. Ian Selley was away on England youth duty in Australia so Paul Davis stepped up for his first League game in 14 months. Ruel Fox fired the Canaries in front. Ian Wright had a penalty saved then struck the 82nd minute goal that rescued a point.

SENT TO COVENTRY

It was ten days before the next outing, at Coventry. Adams had returned. Wright played knowing another booking would cost him an F.A. Cup semi-final place.

Davis found Kevin Campbell to put Arsenal ahead after 28 minutes. Wright added a second within a minute to seize the points but had to go off after an hour giving rise to talk of a hernia operation.

Southampton's visit brought seven goals and a match-winning performance from Jimmy Carter. The winger scored to make it 3-1

for the Gunners after 20 minutes – then smacked the winner from sub David Hillier's quick free kick, after Saints had pulled back to 3-3.

Fears about Wright receded as he returned for the trip to Manchester United. United made most of the running but Peter Schmeichel was kept busy and the United fans were relieved when Paul Merson's 30-yard lob cannoned off the bar with Schmeichel beaten.

PREMIER LEAGUE RESULTS

MARCH 1

| Chelsea 1 | Arsenal 0 |
| Stuart | |

MARCH 3

| Norwich City 1 | Arsenal 1 |
| Fox | Wright |

MARCH 13

| Coventry City 0 | Arsenal 2 |
| | Campbell, Wright |

MARCH 20

Arsenal 4	Southampton 3
Carter 2	Dowie, Adams
Linighan, Merson	Le Tissier

MARCH 24

| Manchester Utd. 0 | Arsenal 0 |

LEAGUE POSITION

Pld	W	D	L	F	A	Pts	Pos
33	13	8	12	33	30	47	9th

ARSENAL
support Great Gunner
Michael

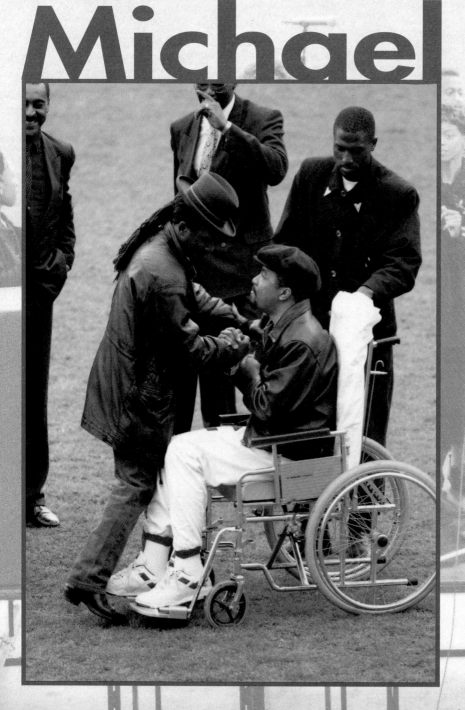

BELOW LEFT: Aswad's Brinsley Forde greets Michael Watson, watched by Kevin Campbell.

MAIN PICTURE: The London Community Gospel Choir.

BELOW RIGHT: Liam Brady, back in an Arsenal shirt, in the 7-2 win over Old Spurs.

Arsenal staged one of the most moving events of the year, when Highbury hosted the Michael Watson Benefit Day on March 28. The 18,000-plus crowd was a fitting tribute to a great Gunner.

Arsenal weren't sure exactly how many fans were going to turn up. The original plan was to open the East Stand. Then the West Stand was filled. Eventually the Clock End was opened to fit in everyone else who had arrived.

The afternoon began with a match between the Arsenal ex-pro and celebrity team and an 'all-star' line-up put together by Michael's representative, Ambrose Mendy. Watson was one of the founder-members of the Gunners' charity squad, and proudly played several games in the red-and-white shirt.

The day continued with Arsenal Ladies pipping Doncaster Belles 2-1 in the crucial women's National Premier League clash. Then a team of Arsenal greats beat their Tottenham counterparts 7-2 in the main event – a result to delight Michael.

Said Mendy: 'The doctors say Michael will never walk again, and he is paralysed down his left side. But he can speak and he is very alert mentally. It was always his dream to fight at Highbury. He was overwhelmed by the benefit at Arsenal.'

CHARITY DINNER

Aswad, Chrissie Hynde and the London Community Gospel Choir supported Michael's big day. So did stars of showbiz and boxing. The evening charity dinner in Michael's honour was a sell-out. And the applause the ex-world middleweight title contender received as he was wheeled around Highbury by Kevin Campbell showed how highly he's regarded by the Arsenal fans.

'There's only one Michael Watson,' chanted the North Bank before his fateful contest with Chris Eubank at Tottenham. On March 28, Arsenal fans proved that wasn't an idle boast.

George Graham wants to be ranked among the great Arsenal managers. He's already claimed his place by leading the Gunners to two league titles. But that's not enough for George. He wants to build a Highbury dynasty to compare with the legendary Herbert Chapman's success in the 1930s.

RIGHT: Champions and 'Manager of the Season' – two trophies for George in 1991.

BELOW: George Graham in the dug-out with chief coach Stewart Houston.

Graham's obsession with Arsenal stretches far beyond the pitch. His Highbury office is lined with portraits of Arsenal's title-winning managers and he's a devoted collector of Gunners memorabilia. Whenever there's an auction with Arsenal involved, George will be there.

'I enjoyed my best days here as a player and I've never forgotten the standards Arsenal set,' says Graham, who revitalised the Gunners after his arrival in May 1986. Cup glory earned George his first success, when Arsenal beat Liverpool 2-1 in the 1987 Littlewoods Cup final.

But two league championships have given him most pleasure. And Arsenal's European Cup exit against Benfica in 1991 was one of his worst moments as a manager.

EUROPEAN AMBITIONS

'I've always wanted to go back into Europe – in whatever competition. But the European Cup is the one that haunts me,' says Graham, who will lead Arsenal's challenge for the European Cup Winners Cup in 1993/4.

'We'd started so well, with a 6-1 win over FK Austria, and a 1-1 draw in Lisbon. Benfica earned the applause that night at Highbury because they finished with such style. But if we'd scored again after Colin Pates gave us the lead, it might have been different. That's why I want another go.'

'Our league form over the last two seasons has hurt my pride. We can do a lot better. That's what I'll be looking for in the year ahead,' says Graham, who wants to become the first Arsenal manager to celebrate three championship wins.

'I've always wanted to go back into Europe –
in whatever competition. But the European
Cup is the one that haunts me.'

GUNNERS LADIES
set the standard

Arsenal Ladies have become the team every women's club wants to beat.

But they'll have a hard job if the treble-winning Gunners maintain the standards they set in 1992/3, when Arsenal deposed Doncaster Belles at the top of the women's game!

Yet, last summer, manager Vic Akers would have settled for a place in the Premier League top three and maybe a cup victory to add to the League Cup of 1991/2.

Instead, Arsenal won the national championship, in their first season in the Premier League; crushed Doncaster 3-0 to lift the WFA Cup for the first time; then succesfully defended the

League Cup with a 3-0 win over Knowsley at Wembley.

'We'd won promotion at a canter and I wasn't sure how we'd cope with the top reaches of the Premier League,' said Akers who'd added England midfielder Debbie Bampton and ex-Ipswich striker Chris Couling to the 1991/2 squad.

THE BELLES SILENCED

'Then we just kept winning and winning . . . and that win over the Belles at Highbury lit up our league campaign.'

Skipper Gill Wylie and colleagues lost just once all season – 0-2 to the Belles at Armthorpe. It seemed goal difference would decide the title. Then Wimbledon drew with Doncaster – and Arsenal seized their chance.

Wylie thundered home an early corner and topscorer Naz Ball clinched a 2-1 victory.

So Akers' squad went into their last league game, at Red Star Southampton, needing one point for the championship. No worries. Ball, Bampton (2), and Jo Churchman all netted before half time for a 4-1 victory.

Meanwhile, Wylie had already lifted the WFA Cup after a 3-0 win over the Belles in the final at Oxford. Goalkeeper Lesley Shipp was voted 'Player-of-the-Match'.

England international Michelle Curley curled in a corner to give Arsenal the lead. Then she crossed for Ball to make it 2-0 in first half injury time. Bampton grabbed the third, after Ball's effort was blocked.

'Now we've set the standards for, we've a lot to live up to in 1993/4,' says Akers.

'The supporters know we're deadly serious and competitive. They look for our results now,' says Wylie.

TOP LEFT: Arsenal Ladies manager and physiotherapist Vic Akers.

ABOVE: A happy team group in the Highbury dressing room, after the 2-1 win over Doncaster.

BOTTOM LEFT: Gill Wylie heads Arsenal in front against Doncaster Belles at Highbury.

COCA COLA

CUP • RUN

Arsenal's run to the Coca Cola Cup final almost floundered at the first hurdle.

First Division Millwall came to Highbury and led 1-0 until 13 minutes from the end, when sub Kevin Campbell snatched a vital equaliser. Ian Wright was flattened by a coin thrown from the Millwall supporters. In the return Campbell put Arsenal ahead after 17 minutes. Millwall levelled through a Lee Dixon own goal. Penalties decided. David Seaman performed heroics, saving three Millwall penalties.

David Hillier, Campbell and Alan Smith scored from the spot and Arsenal edged through.

RAMS REPLAY

Next up were Derby. Arsenal started with Pal Lydersen and Stephen Morrow in place of the injured Lee Dixon and Nigel Winterburn. The atmosphere was hostile. And the Derby crowd went wild when Paul Simpson converted

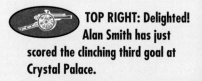

TOP RIGHT: Delighted! Alan Smith has just scored the clinching third goal at Crystal Palace.

BELOW: Ian Wright blasts home a penalty to put Arsenal ahead at Selhurst Park.

BELOW RIGHT: Ian Wright opens the scoring against Nottingham Forest.

a 70th minute penalty. Campbell came to the rescue once more, collecting Anders Limpar's pass to force a replay – five weeks later, because of Derby's Anglo-Italian Cup commitments! Campbell and Ian Wright wrapped that game up early, despite Mark Pembridge's 44th minute penalty for the Rams.

The postponed fourth round tie at Scarborough bordered on farce. The pitch was soaked. Fog enveloped the ground throughout the first half. But Arsenal kept their nerve and Winterburn drilled the only goal.

That brought Nottingham Forest to Highbury. The Gunners upped the tempo after a stuttering first half. Wright's pace terrified the Forest defence. The England striker claimed both goals.

SEMI-FINALS

Wright hit the opener, from the penalty spot, in the semi-final first leg against his old club, Crystal Palace. Alan Smith lashed the sec-ond after Nigel Martyn had blocked Wright. Simon Osborn replied from the spot in the second half, but Smith prodded home Arsenal's third to make the second leg at Highbury a formality. Andy Linighan's early header killed any hopes of a Palace revival at Highbury. Wright's lunge made it 5-1 on aggregate, and the Gunners then cruised through the second half.

COCA COLA CUP RESULTS

SEPTEMBER 22
(second round first leg)

Arsenal 1	Millwall 1
Campbell	Roberts

OCTOBER 7
(second round second leg)

Millwall 1	Arsenal 1
Dixon (own goal)	Campbell
	(Arsenal won 3-1 on penalties)

OCTOBER 28
(third round)

Derby County 1	Arsenal 1
Simpson (pen)	Campbell

DECEMBER 1
(third round replay)

Arsenal 2	Derby County 1
Wright, Campbell	Pembridge (pen)

JANUARY 6
(fourth round)

Scarborough 0	Arsenal 1
	Winterburn

JANUARY 12
(fifth round)

Arsenal 2	Nottingham F. 0
Wright 2	

FEBRUARY 7
(semi-final first leg)

Crystal Palace 1	Arsenal 3
Osborn (pen)	Smith 2, Wright (pen)

MARCH 10
(semi-final second leg)

Arsenal 2	Crystal Palace 0
Linighan, Wright (Arsenal won 5-1 on aggregate)	

COCA COLA

CUP • FINAL

April 18, 1993 will be long remembered as Stephen Morrow's final.

A day of triumph and tragedy for the Northern Ireland international, who cracked the winning goal – then was carried off in agony with a broken arm during the Gunners' after-match celebrations.

Stephen was sent out to mark Owls playmaker John Sheridan, after snuffing out Ipswich's Jason Dozzell and Geoff Thomas of Crystal Palace, in earlier cup ties.

There was no hint of the drama to come as Wednesday settled fastest. Paul Warhurst hit the outside of a post, and worse followed. A free kick was cleared to the edge of the box and American international John Harkes rifled it back past David Seaman.

Paul Merson inspired Arsenal's comeback. It was fitting he should lash the equaliser – a stunning 25-yarder that left Chris Woods stranded. With Morrow sitting tight on Sheridan and Paul Davis passing sweetly, the Gunners began to take control. Kevin Campbell beat Woods from the edge of the box, only to see his shot cannon off the post straight to the grateful 'keeper.

George Graham's half time lecture tightened the Arsenal defence. Andy Linighan and Tony Adams blotted out Warhurst and Mark Bright.

Morrow's magic moment arrived midway through the second half. Palmer miscued his clearance, and in raced the Northern Ireland international, pouncing to crash his first goal for the Gunners. Talk about picking the right moment to score it!

Ian Wright had a goal disallowed for a foul on Viv Anderson. Wednesday brought on David Hirst in a vain attempt to save the game.

CELEBRATIONS TURN TO TRAGEDY

Then to the drama after the final whistle. Morrow was celebrating with skipper Adams, when he tumbled to the turf. Suddenly the players around him realised this was serious. Stephen was wheeled away on a stretcher, an oxygen mask strapped to his face. He was diagnosed as having a broken arm. The operation was performed that night. The injury kept Morrow out for the rest of the season, and took the shine off the Gunners celebrations. Tony Adams, understandably, was too upset to speak to the press.

George Graham summed up the feeling in the camp. 'It was tragic for Stephen, after he'd played so well. He didn't just score the winning goal, he marked an important opponent out of the game,' said Graham. 'It was a freak accident, which left all the players and staff upset.'

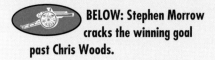

BELOW: Stephen Morrow cracks the winning goal past Chris Woods.

BELOW LEFT: A proud moment. Tony Adams lifts the Coca Cola Cup, supported by David Seaman.

COCA COLA CUP FINAL

Arsenal 2	Sheffield Wed. 1
Merson, Morrow	Harkes

Attendance: 74,007

THE CUPS

APRIL

AFTER THE F.A. CUP Semi-final delirium . . . anti-climax. It was always going to be that way. Middlesbrough on a cold Tuesday night could never compare with Spurs at a packed Wembley.

PREMIER LEAGUE RESULTS

APRIL 6	
Middlesbrough 1	Arsenal 0
Hendrie	

APRIL 10	
Ipswich Town 1	Arsenal 2
Wark (pen)	Smith, Merson

APRIL 12	
Arsenal 0	Aston Villa 1
	Daley

APRIL 21	
Arsenal 1	Nottingham F. 1
Wright	Keane

LEAGUE POSITION

Pld	W	D	L	F	A	Pts	Pos
37	14	9	14	36	34	51	9th

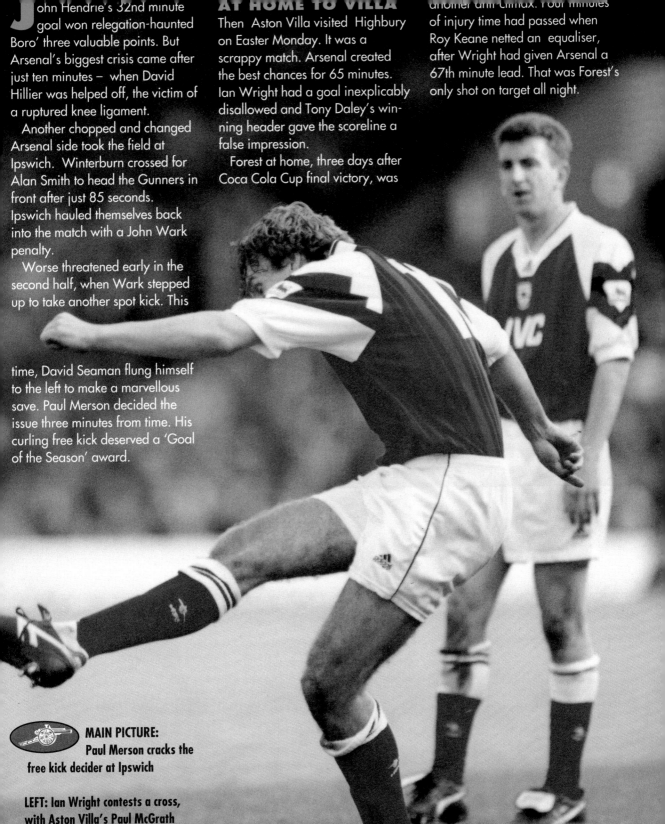

ohn Hendrie's 32nd minute goal won relegation-haunted Boro' three valuable points. But Arsenal's biggest crisis came after just ten minutes – when David Hillier was helped off, the victim of a ruptured knee ligament.

Another chopped and changed Arsenal side took the field at Ipswich. Winterburn crossed for Alan Smith to head the Gunners in front after just 85 seconds. Ipswich hauled themselves back into the match with a John Wark penalty.

Worse threatened early in the second half, when Wark stepped up to take another spot kick. This time, David Seaman flung himself to the left to make a marvellous save. Paul Merson decided the issue three minutes from time. His curling free kick deserved a 'Goal of the Season' award.

AT HOME TO VILLA

Then Aston Villa visited Highbury on Easter Monday. It was a scrappy match. Arsenal created the best chances for 65 minutes. Ian Wright had a goal inexplicably disallowed and Tony Daley's winning header gave the scoreline a false impression.

Forest at home, three days after Coca Cola Cup final victory, was another anti-climax. Four minutes of injury time had passed when Roy Keane netted an equaliser, after Wright had given Arsenal a 67th minute lead. That was Forest's only shot on target all night.

MAIN PICTURE:
Paul Merson cracks the
free kick decider at Ipswich

LEFT: Ian Wright contests a cross,
with Aston Villa's Paul McGrath

THE EYES ON HORIZON

AS THE F.A. CUP final loomed, Arsenal's remaining Premier League fixtures took a back seat. David Hillier and Stephen Morrow were already ruled out for Wembley. George Graham did not want any more injuries.

The Gunners had five matches to negotiate, in ten days. What a way to warm up for English football's major showpiece!

The ordeal began with a meaningless 0-0 draw at Everton, notable only for Steve Bould's return after a troublesome thigh injury. Graham described the game as 'instantly forgettable'.

Tuesday night against QPR wasn't much better. Kevin Campbell went closest for the Gunners. QPR's goalkeeper Tony Roberts made three flying saves. Alan Miller and winger Neil Heaney started for the first time. But everyone knew the Gunners' minds were already at Wembley.

Graham's selection at Sheffield Wednesday two days later demonstrated the farce of the fixture list. None of his line-up would start in the Cup final nine days later.

Scotland U-21 defender Scott Marshall made his full debut and 17-year-old youth utility player Gavin McGowan (a veteran of three reserve appearances!) came on as sub.

PALACE SUFFER

With relegation issues to be decided, Graham had to field his strongest team against Crystal Palace. Ian Wright returned after a broken toe. Ray Parlour and Nigel Winterburn proved their fitness for Wembley too.

Wright fired Arsenal into a ninth minute lead. A

crashing finish by sub Paul Dickov, and a mis-hit Campbell effort – the least he deserved after his bad luck in front of goal – consigned Palace to Division One.

The scoreline caused little joy in the Highbury dressing room. 'I felt sad for Steve Coppell, who'd done such a good job for Palace,' said Graham. 'I was hoping they'd stay up, and there was sadness among our players afterwards, because many of them are friends with Palace lads.'

The biggest plus was bustling 20-year-old Dickov. Graham compared him to another 'tenacious Scot' – David Speedie.

Dickov grabbed the limelight again the following Tuesday, against Spurs – still smarting after their Wembley semi-final defeat.

Graham fielded a virtual 'shadow' side. That upset many fans, who wanted the Gunners' strongest team to face the old enemy. The Arsenal boss had

BELOW LEFT: Paul Dickov, who scored brilliant goals against Crystal Palace and Tottenham.

BELOW RIGHT: Ian Wright was voted Capital Gold's 'London Player of the Year' – and collected his trophy (from Terry Venables!) before the game against Spurs.

a ready answer: 'I want to be sure of sending out my first choice side at Wembley.'

Teddy Sheringham and John Hendry gave Spurs a two goal lead. Dickov smacked another cracker to lift Arsenal's hopes – then extinguished by Hendry 12 minutes from time. It was a sad way to end the League season.

PREMIER LEAGUE RESULTS

MAY 1	
Everton 0	Arsenal 0

MAY 4	
Arsenal 0	QPR 0

MAY 6	
Sheffield Wed. 1 Bright	Arsenal 0

MAY 8	
Arsenal 3 Wright, Dickov Campbell	Crystal Palace 0

MAY 11	
Arsenal 1 Dickov	Tottenham H. 3 Sheringham Hendry 2

FINAL LEAGUE RECORD

Pld	W	D	L	F	A	Pts	Pos
42	15	11	16	40	38	56	10th

A DEMANDING Season

Arsenal staff and players all agree. The English season is too wearing. Demands on the top players must be reduced. Arsenal have long campaigned for a maximum 18 club Premier League.

THE GUNNERS were one of only three clubs to oppose the re-introduction of a 22-club top division. Said vice-chairman David Dein: 'We want quality rather than quantity.'

Manager George Graham has repeatedly called for an elite of 16 to 18 clubs. Long before the Gunners' ridiculous four-games-in-a-week end to the Premier League season, the Arsenal boss was attacking the proliferation of fixtures.

'I'd hoped the Premier League would mean fewer matches, so we could have more time to prepare. It hasn't happened. That's about finance, more than football,' said Graham. 'The second half of the season was a case of play-and-rest, play-and-rest, and players don't learn anything that way.'

Physiotherapist Gary Lewin details the medical worries: 'With so many matches on top of each other, there's no time for knocks to heal – and players are more likely to pick up injuries because of the pressure they are under.'

TOO MANY FIXTURES

Arsenal's appearance record holder, David O'Leary, was in the Gunners' squad that played a marathon 70 matches in 1979/80. 'The English fixture list penalises successful clubs. That's the way it's always been,' he said. 'Surely it must change some time.'

'Can you imagine the fixture chaos if we'd been playing in Europe at the same time as reaching two cup finals?' asked skipper Tony Adams, who points out that, including international calls, Arsenal's England stars have played virtually non-stop from August to June.

Alan Smith is one of those England players. He's also the Highbury PFA representative. 'The size of the Premier League must be cut,' he said. 'The demands on the players are too great. The supporters would benefit too, because fresher players could provide better entertainment.'

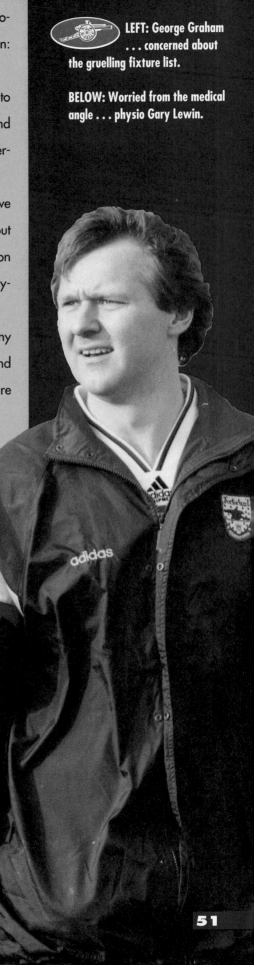

LEFT: George Graham . . . concerned about the gruelling fixture list.

BELOW: Worried from the medical angle . . . physio Gary Lewin.

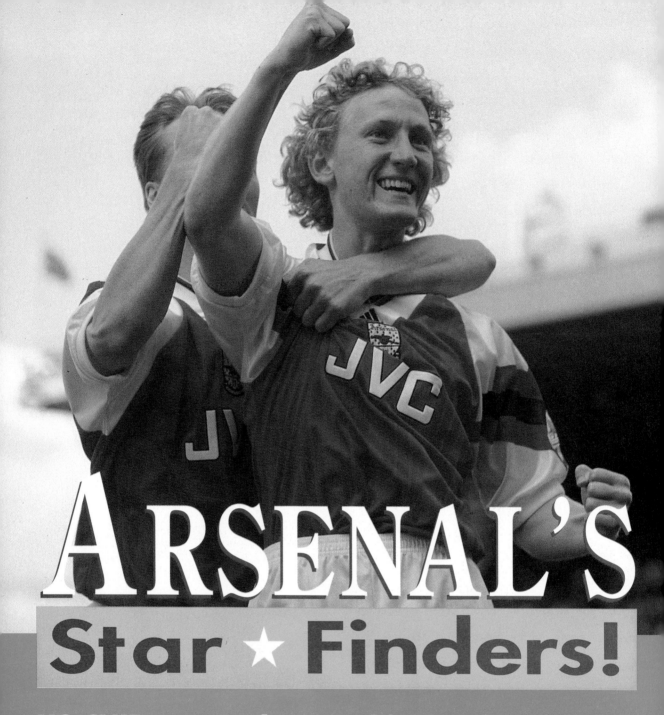

ARSENAL'S
Star ★ Finders!

NO CLUB can match Arsenal in developing home-grown stars who win championships and cups. Every successful Arsenal side of the last 25 years has been built around a nucleus of players who rose through the Gunners' youth ranks.

The 1971 'double' winners contained Pat Rice, Peter Storey, Peter Simpson, George Armstrong, Charlie George, John Radford, Ray Kennedy, Eddie Kelly and Jon Sammels, who'd all been Highbury apprentices.

David O'Leary, Paul Davis, Tony Adams, Paul Merson, David Rocastle and Michael Thomas won championship medals in 1989 and 1991 – along with Martin Hayes in Arsenal's first title campaign plus David Hillier and Kevin Campbell two years ago.

In 1992/3, Ray Parlour, Mark Flatts and Ian Selley made the big breakthrough. Their success is a huge source of pride to chief scout Steve Burtenshaw, and youth officer Terry Murphy, who've nurtured so many stars through their early days at Highbury.

Bargain buys like Lee Dixon, Nigel Winterburn and Steve Bould have also played key roles in Arsenal's title triumphs.

Burtenshaw, Arsenal's first team coach in the early 70s, returned to revise the Gunners scouting operation 13 years ago. Meanwhile, former schoolmaster Murphy looks after youth entrants.

Now Arsenal are expanding their scouting network even further.

Anders Limpar, John Jensen and Pal Lydersen arrived from Scandinavia, and Burtenshaw reckons eastern Europe will soon open up too.

ABILITY AND TEMPERAMENT – THE KEYS

'Obviously players need ability. But they need something more if they're going to make it at Highbury,' says Steve: 'They must have the desire to succeed, and the temperament to go with it, because Arsenal players have to live their lives in a goldfish bowl of attention.

'It's not just a question of finding the right players. An important part of my job is keeping the wrong ones out!'

'Why have we been more successful than most at developing young players? That would need a book to itself,' smiles Terry Murphy. 'We've worked at it longer than most clubs. We have an excellent network of scouts. We're very selective in the boys we sign. We persevere with them for two years at least. Boys know that Arsenal have always given young players their chance. That's a great incentive for youngsters to join us.'

> 'The players must have the desire to succeed, because they have to live their lives in a goldfish bowl of attention.'

 LEFT: Ray Parlour, one of Arsenal's many young stars who started as trainee apprentice.

BELOW: 'Star finders' Terry Murphy (left) and Steve Burtenshaw (right).

THE ARSENAL MUSEUM

A HIGHBURY SHRINE

Few clubs in the world can match the Gunners glorious history – and the newly-opened Arsenal Museum is a shrine to the club's great traditions.

CURATOR IAIN COOK has spent more than a year preparing to throw open the Museum doors at the start of 1993/4, painstakingly piecing together exhibits and memorabilia from 107 years of history.

Says Iain: 'It's all there: from the first group of munitions workers at Woolwich in 1886, collecting their sixpences to buy their first football, right up to Ian Wright collecting match balls for scoring hat tricks!'

The famous club's beginnings were humble. The early Gunners flirted with the First Division and flitted around Woolwich and Plumstead until the dramatic move to Highbury in 1913. Herbert Chapman's arrival in 1925 set Arsenal on the road to glory. Great players became Arsenal's trademark – Alex James,

Cliff Bastin, Eddie Hapgood, George Male, Joe Hulme, David Jack, Ted Drake, Jack Crayston.

Those terrific 1930's successes are covered every inch of the way in the Museum collection, along with the achievements of Tom Whittaker's post-war champions, Bertie Mee's 'double' team, and George Graham's current squad.

The Museum isn't just a matter of record. It tells Arsenal's thrilling story in unconventional ways.

Find out about the great figures who've shaped the club, the trophies they won and the memorabilia they collected; watch Arsenal's history unfold in the audio-visual theatre, plot the change in kit fashions, discover and share an open top bus with your favourite stars as they parade in triumph. They're all at the Arsenal Museum!

The Arsenal Museum is sited on the first floor of the new North Bank Stand. Museum entry will be free to Bond holders. Otherwise, entry costs £2 (£1 for U-16s and senior citizens). There is full disabled access to the Museum. The Museum also features in the club's new Stadium Tour, along with visits to: the press rooms, directors box, original trophy cabinets, boardroom, dressing rooms, the marble halls, players' tunnel and the new North Bank Stand. Tours last two hours and cost £4 (£2 for U-16s and senior citizens).

FROM YEOVIL TO

WEMBLEY

It started at Yeovil and ended at Wembley . . . Yet few would have bet on the Gunners on the basis of their League form.

When Arsenal won the double in 1971, they began their F.A. Cup procession at Yeovil. Now, press, TV and radio gathered, sensing an upset to make national headlines. 'Sorry to disappoint you, lads,' grinned George Graham after Ian Wright's hat trick had demolished the friendly Somerset non-leaguers.

LEEDS AGAIN

The fourth round matched Arsenal with Leeds in a re-run of the marathon 1991 tie. It looked all over bar the shouting when Leeds led 2-0 at half time. The Gunners came out blazing in the second half. Ray Parlour quickly pulled one back. Then, with nine minutes left, Paul Merson unleashed a magical 25-yarder that flashed past keeper John Lukic.

So to a replay at Elland Road. Injury-hit Arsenal arrived with youngsters Ian Selley, Ray Parlour and Stephen Morrow in midfield. It looked like a backs-to-the-wall job. David Seaman made a breathtaking early save from Lee Chapman. Yet the longer the game went on, the more comfortable the battling Gunners seemed.

Leeds were stunned when Ian Wright crossed from the left and Alan Smith hooked Arsenal in front. The lead didn't last. Carl Shutt and Gary McAllister made it 2-1 for Leeds. Up popped Wright again with the minutes ticking away. Extra time – and Wright cracked the third. Arsenal will rarely score a gutsier win.

Two more Wright corkers – both from Ian Selley 'assists' – saw off Nottingham Forest in the fifth round.

SIXTH ROUND

On to Ipswich for the quarter-final. Tony Adams hadn't scored since March 1992. The Arsenal skipper, playing with a dressing on his forehead, headed home Merson's free kick to equalise Chris Kiwomya's opener.

The Gunners turned the screw after the interval. John Wark floored Wright in the box, and Ian stroked away the penalty. Then Phil Whelan, under pressure from Wright, nicked a back pass past Clive Baker. Bontcho Guentchev made it 3-2 when Arsenal failed to clear a free kick. But sub Kevin Campbell cracked a fourth in the dying minutes.

Now for Tottenham at Wembley!

F.A. CUP RESULTS

JANUARY 2 (third round)	
Yeovil Town 1 Batty (pen)	Arsenal 3 Wright 3

JANUARY 25 (fourth round)	
Arsenal 2 Parlour, Merson	Leeds United 2 Speed, Chapman

FEBRUARY 3 (fourth round replay, after extra time)	
Leeds United 2 Shutt, McAllister	Arsenal 3 Smith, Wright 2

FEBRUARY 13 (fifth round)	
Arsenal 2 Wright 2	Nottingham F. 0

MARCH 6 (sixth round)	
Ipswich Town 2 Kiwomya, Guentchev	Arsenal 4 Adams, Wright (pen), Whelan (own goal), Campbell

This was north London's own cup final – and sweet revenge for Arsenal after Tottenham had denied them a 'double' in 1991.

A crowd of 76,263 packed Wembley on April 4. The taunting came from the Tottenham end, harking back to their 3-1 Semi-Final victory in 1991.

Tony Adams said, 'Everyone who played then knows it was one of the worst days of our careers. That gave us a little extra incentive.'

'Sitting in the dressing room, knowing we'd lost to Spurs was the worst feeling I've experienced as a footballer,' said Nigel Winterburn.

Tottenham had caught Arsenal cold with two early goals in 1991. It didn't happen again. 'George Graham told us to start fast and put them under pressure. We settled quicker and created a couple of half chances,' said Kevin Campbell.

That early effort took its toll. 'We'd expended a lot of energy and Spurs came right back into it in the 20 minutes before half time,' said Campbell.

Tottenham claimed a penalty when Andy Linighan challenged Darren Anderton – outside the box. David Seaman was immaculate as Spurs stepped up the pressure.

'I was glad to get to the boys at half time with the score still 0-0,' recalled George Graham. The second half was a different story.

'They needed to score when they had their good spell,' said Ray Parlour. 'They didn't and we started to get on top.'

ADAMS DECIDES IT

Erik Thorstvedt made great saves from Ian Selley and Ian Wright; Wright screwed wide from close range. With 13 minutes left, Adams turned the tie. Gary Mabbutt and Neil Ruddock sandwiched Parlour on the edge of the box. Merson swung over the free kick. The Gunners skipper arrived on the far post to head the winner.

Arsenal played the closing minutes without Lee Dixon, sent off for a second bookable offence. They held on to win.

MAIN PICTURE: Tony Adams heads home Paul Merson's free kick for the only goal of the game.

BOTTOM LEFT: Tony is engulfed by happy Gunners Ray Parlour, Andy Linighan, Ian Wright and Kevin Campbell.

F.A. CUP SEMI-FINAL

Arsenal 1	Tottenham H. 0
Adams	

Attendance: 76,263

ROUND ONE!

Spectacle had fled the 1993 F.A. Cup final. Two weary teams produced a tired contest.

Wednesday started fast. David Seaman made brilliant saves from Carlton Palmer's near post header and Chris Waddle's 30-yard free kick.

In between, Andy Linighan couldn't reach Paul Merson's corner to convert a free header.

WRIGHT ON TARGET

After 18 minutes, Paul Warhurst's error let in Ian Wright, but Chris Woods saved his shot. Three minutes later, Mark Bright brought down Lee Dixon, Paul Davis floated the free kick, Linighan nodded it across goal and Wright stooped to nod Arsenal ahead.

The Gunners tightened their grip. John Jensen snuffed out whoever came into his area. At half time, the odds were on the Gunners.

Then, for 20 minutes, the Owls played their smartest football. David Hirst headed wide, then had a shot blocked. An equaliser seemed inevitable. A John Sheridan cross was nodded back by Bright, and John Harkes stooped at the far post to touch the ball into Hirst's path.

Arsenal brought on Alan Smith, and

F.A. CUP FINAL

Arsenal 1	Sheffield Wed. 1
Wright	Hirst

Arsenal: Seaman, Dixon, Winterburn, Davis, Linighan, Adams, Jensen, Wright (O'Leary, 90 minutes), Campbell, Merson, Parlour (Smith, 65 minutes)

Arsenal again wore squad numbers rather than 1 to 11

Attendance: 79,347

grew stronger as the minutes wore on. Goalmouth action continued to be sparse. Yet Woods made a magnificent last minute save from Wright's ferocious volley.

Even extra time couldn't produce a winner. David O'Leary came on for the injured Wright. George Graham used him as a sweeper, pushing Dixon and Nigel Winterburn into midfield.

Long shots by Roland Nilsson and Dixon were all that bothered the goalkeepers.

So, to a replay on Thursday . . .

THE GUNNERS FIND A NEW HERO

Andy Linighan . . . folk hero! Who'd have believed it in January?

F.A. CUP REPLAY

Arsenal 2   **Sheffield Wed. 1**
Wright, Linighan   Waddle

Arsenal: Seaman, Dixon, Winterburn, Davis, Linighan, Adams, Jensen, Wright (O'Leary, 81 minutes), Smith, Merson, Campbell
   sub not used: Selley

Arsenal again wore squad numbers rather than 1 to 11

Attendance: 62,267

The £1.2 million ex-Norwich defender was booed off, after a mistake let in Sheffield United to snatch a point on January 9. But on May 20, the Arsenal half of north London belonged to Linighan.

Outstanding over both legs of the Cup final marathon, he saved us all from the lottery of a penalty shoot-out.

And he did it with a busted nose and a broken finger. Few Wembley winners have shown as much bottle.

IMMACULATE TIMING

Alan Sunderland against Manchester United in 1979; Linighan 14 years later. When the Gunners win the F.A. Cup, they get the timing right!

Extra time should never have been needed. Arsenal dominated the first 65 minutes of a bruising confrontation. Paul Merson had the best early chance, saved by Woods, before Alan Smith – in for Ray Parlour – sent Ian Wright racing through to beat the England 'keeper after 34 minutes.

Smith flicked another effort into the side netting. Wednesday hadn't troubled David Seaman.

That all changed after 68 minutes. Chris Waddle's shot deflected off Lee Dixon and Seaman was beaten.

MAIN PICTURE: How's that for timing? Andy Linighan heads the last minute winner.

ABOVE: The double-cup winners celebrate.

ABOVE LEFT: Ian Wright slots the Gunners in front.

Wednesday were on a high. They could have won it a few minutes later. Mark Bright stubbed a free shot – and it nicked off the outside of a post.

Extra time again . . .

Tired legs tried to conjure up a winner. Penalties looked inevitable. Then Linighan struck – and earned his old club, Norwich, a UEFA Cup place.

Andy had won over his doubters who wondered if he could really replace the injured Steve Bould.

'The biggest help was having a long run in the side. I was able to settle in and settle down,' he recalled. 'The semi-final success over Tottenham and the Coca Cola victory added to my confidence.'

'Andy has had a difficult time at Arsenal. But he's gradually taken his opportunity,' added Graham. 'Now he's a hero, and deservedly so!'

ARSENAL

ROLL OF HONOUR

League Champions:

1931, 1933, 1934, 1935, 1938, 1948, 1953, 1971, 1989, 1991

Runners-up: **1926, 1932, 1973**

F.A. Cup Winners:

1930, 1936, 1950, 1971, 1979, 1993

Runners-up: **1927, 1932, 1952, 1972, 1978, 1980**

League Cup Winners:

1987, 1993

Runners-up: **1968, 1969, 1988**

European Fairs Cup Winners:

1970

European Cup Winners Cup:

Runners-up: **1980**